I'M NOT ANTI-BUSINESS, I'M ANTI-IDIOT

A DILBERT® BOOK

BY SCOTT ADAMS

Andrews McMeel
Publishing

Kansas City

3 0073 00297 1175

Blah, blah, blah, Pam. Blah, blah, blah.

Other DILBERT Books from Andrews McMeel Publishing

Seven Years of Highly Defective People
ISBN: 0-8362-3668-8

Casual Day Has Gone Too Far
ISBN: 0-8362-2899-5

Fugitive from the Cubicle Police
ISBN: 0-8362-2119-2

Still Pumped from Using the Mouse
ISBN: 0-8362-1026-3

It's Obvious You Won't Survive By Your Wits Alone
ISBN: 0-8362-0415-8

Bring Me the Head of Willy the Mailboy!
ISBN: 0-8362-1779-9

Shave the Whales
ISBN: 0-8362-1740-3

Dogbert's Clues for the Clueless
ISBN: 0-8362-1737-3

Build a Better Life by Stealing Office Supplies
ISBN: 0-8362-1757-8

Always Postpone Meetings with Time-Wasting Morons
ISBN: 0-8362-1758-6

For ordering information, call 1-800-642-6480.

Introduction

I'm a misunderstood cartoonist.

The people who misunderstand me the most are the ones who write to tell me they enthusiastically agree with my opinions. Those people scare me. Sometimes they develop irrational attractions to me, based on the fact that our opinions are so similar. They often inquire about the possibilities of mating with me, or—if they are male—drugging me and keeping me in a basement in a big glass container. It's all very flattering.

Other people write to tell me they plan to hunt me down and beat me senseless with ceramic statues because my opinions are at odds with their own well-constructed views of the universe. The people who worship unicorns come to mind. They're a vindictive group.

Still other people call me a hypocrite because their incomplete information about my actions is inconsistent with their misinterpretation of my opinions. I deal with this the only way I know how to—by signing their names to anti-unicorn literature.

The problem with other people's opinions about my opinions is that no one actually knows my opinions. All anyone knows about me is the dialogue I put in the mouths of rotund engineers, talking rats, megalomaniac dogs, and pointy-haired bosses. I might be dumb, but I'm not dumb enough to express my true opinion about anything important. The one thing I've learned about freedom of expression is that you really ought to keep that sort of thing to yourself.

That said, I do feel an irrational need to make one futile attempt to clear up the biggest misconception about my opinions: I'm not anti-*management*. I'm anti-*idiot*. The two groups intersect so often that I use the terms interchangeably, even though I know I shouldn't. Let me set the record straight: If you think you're a smart manager, you have my word that I'm only making fun of other people.*

Sincerely,

S.Adams

Scott Adams

*Unless you worship unicorns.

THE COMPANY HAS DECIDED TO OUTSOURCE ALL OF THE FUNCTIONS THAT WE'RE NOT ANY GOOD AT.

Yippee! Yay!

WHEN'S YOUR LAST DAY?

UH-OH... THEY'RE NOT GOOD AT KNOWING WHAT THEY'RE NOT GOOD AT...

I DON'T UNDERSTAND WHY SOME PEOPLE WASH THEIR BATH TOWELS.

WHEN I GET OUT OF THE SHOWER I'M THE CLEANEST OBJECT IN MY HOUSE. IN THEORY, THOSE TOWELS SHOULD BE GETTING CLEANER EVERY TIME THEY TOUCH ME.

MAYBE I COULD HUG YOU EVERY DAY SO I DON'T NEED TO TAKE SHOWERS.

ARE TOWELS SUPPOSED TO BEND?

I'VE GOTTA RUN TO THE POST OFFICE.

YOU GO TO THE POST OFFICE EVERY DAY. ARE YOU AWARE THAT YOU CAN BUY MORE THAN ONE STAMP AT A TIME?

APPARENTLY YOU DON'T UNDERSTAND THE CONCEPT OF "FLOAT."

S. Adams

© 1995 United Feature Syndicate, Inc. (NYC)

8

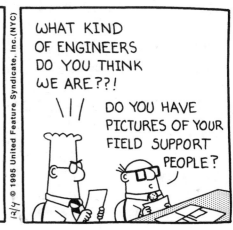

SO, YOU IGNORED MY RECOMMENDATION AND BOUGHT A LOW-COST SYSTEM THAT'S TOTALLY INADEQUATE...

YOU COMPENSATED FOR THIS BLUNDER BY MAKING IT PART OF MY OBJECTIVES TO MAKE THE SYSTEM WORK...

YOU'LL GET A BONUS FOR SAVING MONEY. I'LL GET FIRED, THUS SAVING MORE MONEY AND EARNING YOU ANOTHER BONUS.

I'M ON A ROLL.

IT'S FUNNY — BEFORE YOUR COMPANY BOUGHT THAT CRITICAL SYSTEM FROM ME, YOU HAD ALL THE POWER...

BUT NOW, ONLY I CAN PROVIDE ESSENTIAL UPGRADES!! I CALL THE SHOTS, YOU SIMPLE FOOL!!

SEND IN THE NEXT EMPLOYEE.

AT LEAST WE DON'T HAVE ANY MULTI-VENDOR COMPATIBILITY ISSUES.

IT'S INEXPLICABLE, BUT THE LOW-COST SYSTEM I SOLD YOU SEEMS TO BE WOEFULLY UNDER-POWERED.

YOU COULD REPLACE IT WITH ANOTHER VENDOR'S SYSTEM, THUS SHOWING EVERYBODY YOU MADE A MISTAKE. OR YOU CAN PAY MY OUTRAGEOUS UPGRADE FEES.

HOW BIG A FOOL DO YOU THINK I AM?

I WON'T KNOW UNTIL I SEE IF YOU GO FOR THE LEASE OPTION.

© 1995 United Feature Syndicate, Inc.(NYC)

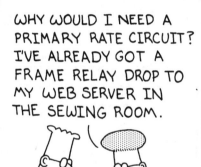

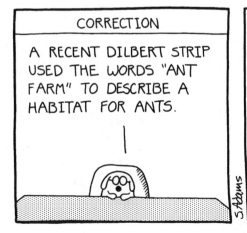

A WHILE BACK I ASKED FOR OPINIONS ABOUT THIS NEW CHARACTER, "TINA THE BRITTLE TECH WRITER."

RRRR

RESULTS

MOST PEOPLE, INCLUDING NEARLY ALL SELF-DESCRIBED FEMINISTS, SAID KEEP HER. BUT THERE WERE MANY REQUESTS TO ADD "NON-STEREOTYPICAL" FEMALE CHARACTERS FOR BALANCE.

IN THE INTEREST OF BALANCE I GIVE YOU "ANTINA."

IS ANYBODY UP FOR SOME MATH?

HI, I'M ANTINA THE NON-STEREOTYPICAL WOMAN.

THAT COMPUTER MONITOR YOU'RE USING IS SUPPOSED TO BE 17 INCHES. BUT IT'S MORE LIKE 16.5 INCHES.

I TOOK THE COFFEE MACHINE APART JUST FOR FUN— WANT TO SEE?

I'VE DECIDED TO MASK MY BOYISH LOOKS BY GROWING A BEARD.

I DIDN'T THINK TED WAS SMART ENOUGH TO KNOW HOW TO GROW A BEARD.

HEE HEE

TWO WEEKS LATER

HOW DO YOU LIKE MY BEARD?

MY SEARCH FOR A NEW MANAGER IS OVER.

I PROMOTED TED TO BE YOUR NEW MANAGER. I USED TO THINK HE LOOKED BOYISH, BUT HIS NEW BEARD CHANGED THAT.

ARE EITHER OF YOU THE LEAST BIT CONCERNED THAT TED'S BEARD IS GROWING FROM HIS FOREHEAD?

SHE MADE IT SOUND AS IF IT'S WRONG.

YOU CAN PUNISH THEM FOR HAVING BAD OPINIONS.

1/4/96

AS YOUR NEW BOSS I HAVE YET TO SELECT MY "PET" EMPLOYEE. I SHALL DO THIS BY CLOSING MY EYES AND POINTING THE BEARD ON MY FOREHEAD.

TO MAKE IT FAIR, I'LL CLOSE MY EYES WHILE ONE OF YOU SPINS MY CHAIR!

1/5/96

STAIRS

ALICE...UM... TECHNICALLY THIS ISN'T "SPINNING."

HOW DO YOU LIKE BEING A MANAGER, TED?

YESTERDAY MY STAFF PUSHED ME DOWN TEN FLIGHTS OF STAIRS. MY SOUL LEFT MY BODY AND NOW I'M A LIFELESS EVIL ENTITY.

1/6/96

JUST IN TIME TO DO PERFORMANCE REVIEWS!

I COULDN'T HAVE PLANNED IT BETTER.

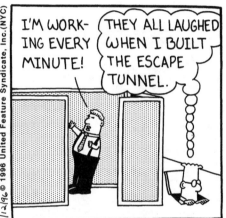

THE COMPANY ANNOUNCED A NEW COMPENSATION PLAN TODAY. BONUSES WILL BE PAID ONLY TO THE TOP TEN PERCENT OF THE EMPLOYEES.

IN RELATED NEWS, 89% OF THE EMPLOYEES RESIGNED IN BITTER DISGUST. THE TOP TEN PERCENT ALSO LEFT, REALIZING THEY COULD GET BETTER JOBS ELSE-WHERE.

THIS COULD HAVE AN IMPACT ON THOSE OF YOU WHO REMAIN.

WE GET THE BONUSES?

I'M INVENTING A NEW TECHNOLOGY TO PREVENT KIDS FROM SEEING SMUT ON THE INTERNET.

SO, YOU'RE PITTING YOUR INTELLIGENCE AGAINST THE COLLECTIVE SEX DRIVE OF ALL THE TEENAGERS WHO OWN COMPUTERS?

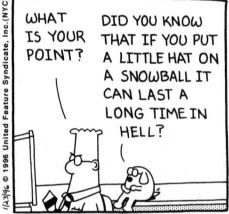

WHAT IS YOUR POINT?

DID YOU KNOW THAT IF YOU PUT A LITTLE HAT ON A SNOWBALL IT CAN LAST A LONG TIME IN HELL?

MATT, YOUR JOB IS TO TEST MY NEW INVENTION THAT BLOCKS KIDS FROM SEEING DIRTY PICTURES ON THE INTERNET.

HIS YOUTHFUL CURIOSITY IS NO MATCH FOR MY TECHNICAL BRILLIANCE.

I HOPE THAT WASN'T THE SOUND OF EYEBALLS GETTING REALLY BIG.

WE WON THE BID TO REBUILD OUR NATION'S AIR TRAFFIC CONTROL SYSTEMS.

YIPPEEE!!! YES!! TO THE PHONES!

THEY DON'T USUALLY GET THAT EXCITED.

BUY A THOUSAND SHARES OF "BLUEHOUND BUS LINES."

I HIRED THE "DOGBERT CONSULTING COMPANY" TO LEAD THE PROJECT BECAUSE NONE OF YOU IS BRIGHT ENOUGH.

AND YOU ALL HAVE BAD ATTITUDES FOR NO APPARENT REASON; THAT'S NO WAY TO BE A LEADER.

SHALL WE GO AROUND THE TABLE AND INTRODUCE OURSELVES?

I DON'T GET CHUMMY WITH THE LOCALS.

WALLY WRITES THE CRITICAL CODE FOR OUR NATION'S NEW AIR TRAFFIC CONTROL SYSTEM.

THE CROWD IS SILENT.

SUDDENLY THE GIFTED PROGRAMMER EMPLOYS A RARELY SEEN STRATEGY OF "CODE REUSE."

THE CROWD GOES WILD.

SO YOU USED CODE FROM THE PAYROLL SYSTEM?

HERE'S A TIP: DON'T FLY ON PAY DAY.

THANKS TO MY LEADER-SHIP, THE NEW AIR TRAFFIC CONTROL SYSTEM IS DESIGNED ON TIME AND UNDER BUDGET.

I HAD TO CUT A FEW CORNERS. THIS BIG RADAR-LOOKING THING IS A WALL CLOCK. AND MOST OF THE BUTTONS ARE GLUED ON.

IT LOOKS LIKE IT MIGHT BE UM... DANGEROUS.

GREAT... I FINISH EARLY AND WHAT DO I GET: "FEATURE CREEP."

I NEED EVERYBODY TO HELP IN THE SHIPPING DEPART-MENT TODAY.

EVERY PRODUCT THAT SHIPS BEFORE THE END OF THE MONTH GETS COUNTED AS REVENUE FOR THE FISCAL YEAR. UNFORTUNATELY, WE DON'T HAVE INVENTORY.

SO WE'LL SHIP WHATEVER IS LYING AROUND, BOOK IT AS REVENUE AND SORT IT OUT LATER.

THIS ONE'S GETTING GUM.

HEY, WALLY! THE BOSS SENT HIS FIRST E-MAIL MESSAGE!

AND YOU SAID HE WASN'T BRIGHT ENOUGH TO FIGURE OUT HOW TO USE E-MAIL!

WHAT'S HIS MESSAGE?

"I FORGOT MY WATCH. DOES ANYBODY KNOW WHAT TIME IT IS?"

TIME TO CHANGE JOBS.

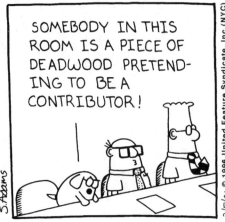

Panel 1: I TOLD YOU THIS PROJECT WOULD TAKE A YEAR. BUT ON MY OBJECTIVES YOU SAY I MUST HAVE IT DONE IN THREE MONTHS.

Panel 2: WHICH OF THESE REASONS BEST DESCRIBES WHY:
A. YOU HAVE GREAT CONFIDENCE IN ME.
B. YOU THINK I PADDED MY ESTIMATE.
C. YOU HATE MY GUTS.

Panel 3: WE DON'T REALLY NEED THE PROJECT. IT'S JUST A WAY TO KEEP RAISES LOW.

I JUST FELT A LITTLE DIP IN MY MOTIVATION.

Panel 4: WALLY, I'VE DECIDED TO MOVE YOUR PROJECT DUE DATE UP A MONTH.

Panel 5: EVERY TIME IT LOOKS LIKE I'LL REACH AN OBJECTIVE, YOU MOVE IT! WHAT DOES THIS PROVE ABOUT MY PERFORMANCE?

Panel 6: IT PROVES I'M BETTER AT SETTING OBJECTIVES THAN YOU ARE AT ACHIEVING THEM.

Panel 7: I HAVE TOO MANY PASSWORDS IN MY LIFE. WHAT IF I FORGET THEM?

Panel 8: YOU'D LOSE YOUR JOB! YOU WOULDN'T BE ABLE TO WITHDRAW MONEY OR CHECK PHONE MESSAGES! YOU'D BE DEAD IN A WEEK!!

Panel 9: THAT WOULD HAVE BEEN A GOOD TIME TO BE QUIETLY SUPPORTIVE, DOGBERT.

OH, YEAH, THAT'S A LOT OF FUN.

CATBERT THE EVIL HUMAN RESOURCES DIRECTOR

THE EMPLOYEES HAVE TOO MUCH TIME OFF. IT MUST BE STOPPED.

I SUMMON THE DEMONS OF DARKNESS TO ASSIST ME!!!

...ELIMINATE SICK DAYS. MAKE THEM USE VACATION DAYS WHEN THEY'RE ILL. CALL IT A "TIME BANK."

IT'S PLAYFUL... IT'S CRUEL... I LIKE IT.

I KNOW I SHOULD BE OFF TORMENTING PEOPLE...

BUT I CAN'T PRY MYSELF AWAY FROM THIS MOST EXCELLENT BUTT-WARMING DEVICE.

IT'S PROBABLY BECAUSE OF THE HYPE, BUT I'M THINKING THIS WOULD BE EVEN BETTER WITH "WINDOWS 95."

AS A CO-OP EMPLOYEE, YOU CAN'T EXPECT THE SAME LUSH CUBICLE ENVIRONMENT THAT THE REGULAR EMPLOYEES ENJOY.

YOU'LL BE SHARING THIS CUBICLE WITH OUR OTHER CO-OPS.

I HEARD THAT THE NEW CO-OP ONLY LASTED ONE DAY.

HE DIDN'T FIT IN.

45

Panel 1: SOMEWHERE IN ELBONIA

I'VE BEEN ASSIGNED TO CHECK THE SOFTWARE YOU'RE WRITING FOR US UNDER CONTRACT.

Panel 2: THE DOCUMENTATION IS WRITTEN IN OUR OWN ELBONIAN LANGUAGE.

IS THAT A PROBLEM?

Panel 3: THAT'S BETTER THAN I'D HOPED. I WAS AFRAID NOBODY HERE KNEW HOW TO WRITE.

WRITING IS EASY. SOMEDAY WE HOPE TO READ, TOO.

Panel 4: BEFORE I ACCEPT THE SOFTWARE YOU WROTE UNDER CONTRACT, TELL ME WHAT DEVELOPMENT METHODOLOGY YOU USE.

Panel 5: WE HOLD VILLAGE MEETINGS TO BOAST OF OUR SKILLS AND CURSE THE DEVIL-SPAWNED END-USERS.

SOMETIMES WE JUGGLE.

Panel 6: AT THE LAST MINUTE WE SLAM OUT SOME CODE AND GO ROLLER SKATING.

I WOULD FIND THIS HUMOROUS IF NOT FOR THE PIG ON MY BACK.

Panel 7: YOU SAVED ONE MILLION DOLLARS BY HAVING PROGRAMMERS IN ELBONIA WRITE SOFTWARE FOR US.

Panel 8: BUT WE WASTED FOUR MILLION DOLLARS TRYING TO DEBUG THE SOFTWARE.

Panel 9: AND THE ENTIRE STAFF OF OUR QUALITY ASSURANCE GROUP QUIT TO BECOME MIMES.

LET'S BLAME THE MIMES; THEY WON'T TALK.

S. Adams

© 1996 United Feature Syndicate, Inc. (NYC)

50

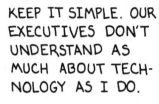
ADD AN EXECUTIVE SUMMARY TO THE APPROVAL PAGE.

KEEP IT SIMPLE. OUR EXECUTIVES DON'T UNDERSTAND AS MUCH ABOUT TECHNOLOGY AS I DO.

HOW COULD THEY KNOW LESS THAN YOU DO? YOU HAVEN'T FIGURED OUT HOW TO MAKE YOUR CAR GO UPHILL.

WRONG; I GOT AAA ROAD SERVICE.

I HAVE TO TURN THIS FIFTY-PAGE PROPOSAL INTO A ONE-PARAGRAPH EXECUTIVE SUMMARY FOR OUR CEO. IT'S IMPOSSIBLE.

SIMPLE.

HOW ABOUT "GIVE US THREE MILLION DOLLARS SO WE CAN BUY COOL TECHNOLOGY, PUMP UP OUR RÉSUMÉS AND ESCAPE THIS FESTERING BOIL YOU CALL A COMPANY"?

I FEEL OBLIGATED TO SAY SOMETHING ABOUT OUR CUSTOMERS.

HOW ABOUT "I'M GLAD I'M NOT ONE OF THEM."

COULD YOU DO A DEMO OF THE NEW PRODUCT FOR OUR VP NEXT WEEK?

WELL... THAT WOULD DELAY THE SHIP DATE, LOWER MORALE AND CREATE AN UNENDING DEMAND FOR MORE UNPRODUCTIVE DEMOS...

LOGICALLY, SINCE YOUR OBJECTIVE IS TO SHOW THAT WE'RE DOING VALUABLE WORK...

AND WE'LL NEED A BANNER THAT SAYS "QUALITY."

MYSTERIES REVEALED

HOW DO CEILING TILES GET DAMAGED?

IT BEGINS WITH A LOWLY ENGINEER WHO MAKES A TECHNOLOGY DECISION.

THE ENGINEER WRITES UP HIS RECOMMENDATION.

TEN PAGES.

THE BOSS SUMMARIZES IT FOR THE EXECUTIVE DIRECTOR.

ONE-PAGE SUMMARY.

THE EXECUTIVE DIRECTOR SUMMARIZES IT FOR THE VICE PRESIDENT.

THREE BULLET POINTS...

THE VP SUMMARIZES IT FOR THE PRESIDENT.

NICE NECKTIE.

THANKS. HAVE SOME STOCK OPTIONS.

THE PRESIDENT SEES A CNN REPORT AND MAKES A TECHNOLOGY DECISION.

INTERACTIVE HOLOGRAPHS ARE HOT!

GET ME SOME OF THAT!

THE ENGINEER IS ASSIGNED TO JUSTIFY THE PRESIDENT'S TECHNOLOGY DECISION.

HE TOOK THAT WELL.

OUCH

RATBERT, WE'D LIKE YOU TO BE THE DIRECTOR OF MARKETING FOR THE COMPANY WE'RE STARTING.

OKAY! WHAT DO I DO?

BE AS ANNOYING AND ILLOGICAL AS YOU CAN. WE'LL WHACK YOU IN THE HEAD WITH BALLED-UP SOCKS TO MAKE YOU SHUT UP.

IT'S DEFINITELY BETTER TO BE AN OWNER THAN AN EMPLOYEE.

LET'S LINK HIS SALARY TO EARNINGS! HEE HEE!

THE BUSINESS PLAN FOR YOUR START-UP IS IDIOTIC BUT I'M GOING TO PROVIDE THE VENTURE CAPITAL FUNDING ANYWAY.

WE'LL GENERATE LOTS OF MEDIA HYPE, GO PUBLIC AND MAKE MILLIONS BY SHAFTING GREEDY AND IGNORANT INVESTORS.

THE LATIN WORD FOR "CLOSE YOUR EYES AND OPEN YOUR MOUTH" IS "PROSPECTUS."

THIS IS EXACTLY WHY I'M AFRAID OF DOGS.

WALLY AND I STARTED OUR OWN COMPANY. WE'RE SELLING THE PRODUCT THAT YOU SAID NOBODY WANTS.

SOON WE WILL BE RICH.

WE DO OUR VICTORY JIG IN YOUR FACE.

BA-BUM

WHEN HE SHOWED YOU YOUR EMPLOYMENT AGREEMENT — WHERE YOU GAVE ALL PATENT RIGHTS TO THIS COMPANY — WHAT PART OF THE JIG WERE YOU DOING?

TURBO MOONING.

SOB

58

AT THE RISK OF DYING FROM BOREDOM, I MUST INTERVIEW YOU FOR THE DEPARTMENT NEWSLETTER.

LET ME GIVE YOU SOME BACKGROUND BEFORE I TALK ABOUT MY PROJECT...

"THE PROJECT IS GOOD," QUIPPED THE ENGINEER.

...SO THERE I AM IN MY MOM'S FALLOPIAN TUBE...

WALLY, I'M HOPING YOU'LL AGREE TO WRITE ABOUT YOUR PROJECT FOR THE NEWSLETTER...

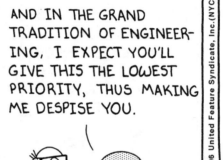

AND IN THE GRAND TRADITION OF ENGINEERING, I EXPECT YOU'LL GIVE THIS THE LOWEST PRIORITY, THUS MAKING ME DESPISE YOU.

SO... ARE YOU SAYING YOU DON'T DESPISE ME NOW?

WE ARE NOT HAVING A "MOMENT" HERE!

PERFORMANCE REVIEW

YOUR MAIN ACCOMPLISHMENT WAS THE DEPARTMENT NEWSLETTER WHICH WAS BOTH UNINTERESTING AND UNIMPORTANT. YOU GET NO RAISE.

THE NEWSLETTER WAS YOUR IDEA, AND IT'S BORING BECAUSE MOST OF THE ARTICLES ARE CONTRIBUTED BY MY IDIOTIC COWORKERS.

YOU DON'T SEEM TO UNDERSTAND THE VALUE OF TEAMWORK.

I UNDERSTAND ITS VALUE; IT JUST COST ME A TWO-PERCENT RAISE.

IN AN EFFORT TO BOOST SALES, LAPTOP COMPUTERS HAVE BEEN GIVEN TO EVERY MEMBER OF THE SALES FORCE.

THAT COULD BE A PROBLEM, GIVEN THE RECENT CUTS TO THE TRAINING BUDGET.

MEANWHILE, IN THE FIELD

AND IF YOU ORDER TODAY, I'LL THROW IN THIS RECTANGULAR PLASTIC THING.

I WISH I HAD AN IVY LEAGUE DEGREE SO I COULD BE PROMOTED TO VICE PRESIDENT.

YOU DON'T NEED ONE.

IT'S IMPOSSIBLE TO BE A VICE PRESIDENT WITHOUT ONE.

I'LL BET $100 I CAN TURN A RAT INTO A VICE PRESIDENT.

THAT WAS GOOD, BUT TRY SAYING IT AS THOUGH YOUR SOUL JUST ABANDONED YOUR BODY.

"WE'VE REORGANIZED TO FOCUS ON OUR CORE COMPETENCY."

REMEMBER EVERYTHING I TAUGHT YOU, RATBERT. IF YOU CAN PASS YOURSELF OFF AS A CORPORATE VICE PRESIDENT, I'LL WIN MY BET.

YO, HEADCOUNT! IF YOU HAVE ANY ISSUES, PUT TOGETHER AN ACTION PLAN. OUR PEOPLE ARE THE BEST. DON'T SPEND MONEY.

DO YOU THINK HE'S REALLY A VICE PRESIDENT?

MAYBE. BUT I'M NOT READY TO RULE OUT "ANNOYING RODENT" YET.

QUALITY.

MISTER RATBERT, I DON'T THINK I CAN HIRE A RAT TO BE OUR VICE PRESIDENT OF MARKETING. YOU NEED EXPERIENCE IN THE TECHNOLOGY INDUSTRY.

I SPENT A WEEK IN A DUMPSTER AT PROCTER AND GAMBLE.

CLOSE ENOUGH! WELCOME TO THE TEAM!

I'LL BRING SOME CRONIES WITH ME. THEY'RE FLIES.

I HAD YEARS OF VALUABLE EXPERIENCE AS A RODENT BEFORE I BECAME VICE PRESIDENT OF MARKETING.

MY MARKETING PLAN IS SIMPLE. EACH OF YOU WILL CLING TO THE LEG OF A TECHNOLOGY COLUMNIST UNTIL WE GET SOME GOOD PRESS.

IT LOOKS LIKE YOU'RE FULL.

YOU CAN CLING TO THE CAT UNTIL A SPACE OPENS.

I QUIT MY JOB AS VICE PRESIDENT OF MARKETING...

I WAS LOSING MY SCRUPLES... BECOMING UNSCRUPULOUS. YES, I LEARNED A VALUABLE LESSON ABOUT SCRUPLES.

AND THAT LESSON WOULD BE?

IT'S FUN TO SAY "SCRUPLES."

TODAY WAS A BAD DAY. FIRST THE VENDING MACHINE STOLE MY MONEY...

...AND BY THE END OF THE DAY I HAD BEEN SENTENCED TO DEATH BY THE DIRECTOR OF HUMAN RESOURCES...

I'VE BECOME TOTALLY DESENSITIZED TO TRAGIC NEWS!

THE EXECUTION IS SCHEDULED FOR TOMORROW. I SHOULD CALL IN SICK.

DOGBERT VERSUS CATBERT

I UNDERSTAND YOU'VE SENTENCED DILBERT TO DEATH.

IS THAT A PROBLEM?

MY ASSISTANT, BOB THE DINOSAUR, WILL NOW DEMONSTRATE HOW TO GIVE A CAT A "FUR WEDGIE."

I'VE BEEN PARDONED. SOMEHOW THEY LOST THE PAPERWORK ORDERING MY EXECUTION.

IT PROBABLY FELL INTO A CRACK.

THE INTERNAL JOB POSTINGS ARE OUT. HERE'S A JOB I'D LOVE.

"EXPERIENCE REQUIRED: THE CANDIDATE MUST BE A GUY NAMED ERIC, POT-BELLIED, NEARSIGHTED, MUST DRIVE A RED FORD BRONCO."

THEY MIGHT HAVE SOMEONE IN MIND ALREADY.

IF I SQUINT... AND LEAVE MY "CONTROL TOP" PANTYHOSE AT HOME...

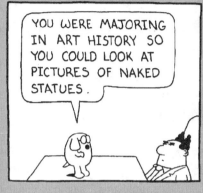

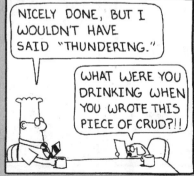

ALICE, YOU'VE BEEN WORKING EIGHTEEN HOURS A DAY. I REALIZED I MUST ADD A PERSON TO THE EFFORT.

SO I HIRED A NIGHT SHIFT MANAGER. AFTER I GO HOME AT FIVE O'CLOCK HE'LL TAKE OVER AND ASK WHY YOU'RE BEHIND SCHEDULE.

I LIKE MY STATUS REPORTS RENDERED IN 3-D, BUT DON'T SPEND A LOT OF TIME ON IT.

THIS DOG IS SPECIALLY TRAINED TO DETECT WASTED RESOURCES.

HE'LL HELP ME FIND OUT WHY YOUR PROJECT IS BEHIND SCHEDULE EVEN AFTER ADDING ME AS MANAGER.

SNIFF SNIFF

WE'LL BEGIN AS SOON AS HE'S DONE PLAYING AROUND.

OH MY! THIS IS SHOCKING!

WHAT?

40% OF ALL SICK DAYS TAKEN BY YOUR STAFF ARE FRIDAYS AND MONDAYS!

WHAT KIND OF IDIOT DO THEY THINK I AM?

NOT AN IDIOT SAVANT. THEY CAN DO MATH.

CATBERT, H.R. DIRECTOR

WALLY, IT MIGHT NOT SEEM FAIR THAT NEW EMPLOYEES ARE PAID MORE THAN YOU...

BUT YOU COULD ALWAYS QUIT AND THEN REAPPLY FOR YOUR OLD JOB AT A HIGHER SALARY.

I JUST MIGHT DO THAT!!

WOULD YOU MIND RUBBING THIS CATNIP ALL OVER YOUR BODY FIRST?

SO I'M THINKING I'LL RESIGN, THEN I'LL REAPPLY FOR MY CURRENT JOB AT A HIGHER SALARY.

THAT'S A GOOD PLAN EXCEPT FOR THE FACT THAT YOU'RE THOROUGHLY UNQUALIFIED FOR YOUR CURRENT JOB.

I NEED TO SHARE MY UNREALISTIC PLANS WITH A FRIEND WHO ISN'T AN ENGINEER.

I'M MORE OF A CO-WORKER THAN A FRIEND, PER SE.

AND THAT'S THE MARKETING PLAN. ANY COMMENTS?

IT APPEARS TO BE A BUNCH OF OBVIOUS GENERALITIES AND WISHFUL THINKING WITH NO APPARENT BUSINESS VALUE.

MARKETING DIDN'T TURN OUT TO BE THE GLAMOUR CAREER I EXPECTED.

I CIRCLED ALL THE WORDS YOU WON'T FIND IN ANY DICTIONARY.

EXPERIMENT #1: I AM EXPOSING A RAT TO MY COMPANY'S MARKETING PLAN.

HE SEEMS TO HAVE NO ADVERSE RESPONSE TO THE INTRODUCTION AND BACKGROUND.

THIS IS ALREADY FAR MORE EXPOSURE THAN HUMANS COULD TOLERATE.

SALES PROJECTIONS...
BRAIN TUMOR...
GET TYLENOL...

HERE'S MY TIME SHEET, INCLUDING GUESSES FOR THE NEXT TWO DAYS SO I CAN MEET YOUR ARBITRARY CLERICAL DEADLINE.

IF ANYTHING IMPORTANT COMES UP, I'LL IGNORE IT TO PRESERVE THE INTEGRITY OF THE TIME-REPORTING SYSTEM.

ARE YOU FINISHED ANNOYING ME YET?

ACCORDING TO MY TIME SHEET I'LL BE HERE FOR ANOTHER 14 MINUTES.

I GOT MYSELF A LITTLE WORK-AVOIDANCE DEVICE.

IF I WANT TO LEAVE A MEETING EARLY, I JUST LOOK DOWN AND SAY "UH-OH" AND SCURRY AWAY.

WHAT'S THE PAGER NUMBER IN CASE I NEED YOU?

YOU'RE NOT QUITE GRASPING THE CONCEPT HERE, ALICE.

75

HERE'S YOUR PROBLEM. THE CONNECTION TO THE NETWORK IS BROKEN.

UH-OH. IT'S A "TOKEN RING" LAN. THAT MEANS THE TOKEN FELL OUT AND IT'S IN THIS ROOM SOMEPLACE.

YOU ARE THE WIND BENEATH MY WINGS.

I'LL WAIT A WEEK THEN TELL HIM THE TOKEN MUST BE IN THE "ETHERNET."

WE'LL HAVE TO ELIMINATE A FEW STEPS IN ORDER TO HIT THE MARKET WINDOW.

I THINK WE CAN GET RID OF MARKET RESEARCH AND TECHNICAL TESTING. THEY'RE BASICALLY "OVERHEAD."

GONE! NOW WE'LL HIT THE WINDOW!

...LIKE A BIRD.

HERE ARE MY BUDGET ESTIMATES FOR THE YEAR.

THANKS TO MANAGEMENT BUNGLING AND INDECISION, I PLAN TO USE NO CAPITAL FOR SEVERAL MONTHS FOLLOWED BY A RECKLESS YEAR-END ORGY OF ACQUISITION.

IS THAT WHAT YOU WERE LOOKING FOR?

TELL ME AGAIN WHAT "CAPITAL" IS.

78

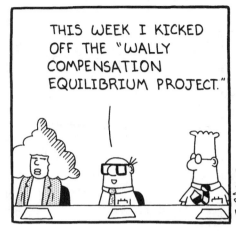

IN THE "DUE DILIGENCE" PHASE OF OUR MERGER YOU WILL GIVE US ACCESS TO ALL OF YOUR PROPRIETARY INFORMATION.

WOULDN'T THAT LET YOU KNOW HOW TO CRUSH US COMPETITIVELY? COULDN'T YOU CANCEL THE MERGER AND TAKE OUR CUSTOMERS WITHOUT PAYING A CENT?

MUST... CONTAIN MANIACAL... LAUGH...

"DUE DILIGENCE" BEFORE THE MERGER.

YOU MUST REVEAL YOUR SECRETS SO MY COMPANY KNOWS WHAT IT'S BUYING.

ALL OF OUR PROJECTS ARE DOOMED. MOST OF THE GOOD EMPLOYEES LEFT. OUR CUSTOMERS ARE STARTING A CLASS ACTION SUIT...

AT LEAST THE BUILDING IS WORTH SOMETHING

IF YOU FEEL A TICKLE, THAT'S ASBESTOS.

WITH ALL THIS TALK OF "DIVERSITY" THERE'S NO MENTION OF THE PAIN WE SMART CREATURES ENDURE WHILE SURROUNDED BY DOLTS.

GOOD POINT. I DON'T KNOW HOW WE DO IT.

IT LOOKS LIKE I'LL HAVE TO HOLD SECRET MEETINGS.

YEAH, OUR LIVES ARE A CONSTANT STRUGGLE.

BUSINESS LANGUAGE EXPLAINED

"WE HAVE TO BE MORE COMPETITIVE."

NICE BARREL.

THIS OLD THING?

MEANING: SAY GOODBYE TO SALARY INCREASES.

"WE MUST FOCUS ON OUR CORE BUSINESS."

HELLO.

MEANING: WE CAN'T FIND OUR BUTTS WITH BOTH HANDS.

"YOU ARE EMPOWERED."

I PROCLAIM THIS TO BE "GREEN INK DAY."

MEANING: YOU'RE THE MONARCH OF UNIMPORTANT DECISIONS.

"WE'RE REENGINEERING YOUR FUNCTION."

MEANING: ADIOS, TONTO, AND THE HORSE YOU RODE IN ON.

"TRAINING IS ESSENTIAL."

YOU WERE A CANNIBAL?

I'M A PEOPLE PERSON.

MEANING: WE'RE TRYING TO HIRE SOME TRAINED PEOPLE.

"WE'RE MARKET DRIVEN."

WHAT'S YOUR FAVORITE ODOR?

RESEARCH

MEANING: WE BLAME CUSTOMERS FOR OUR LACK OF INNOVATION.

"WE VALUE EMPLOYEE INPUT."

THANKS FOR LISTENING.

HA HA HA!

MEANING: WE THINK HUMOR IS IMPORTANT.

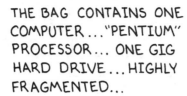
HALT AND SUBMIT TO THE MIND SCAN OF "BRAINITOR, THE GUARDIAN OF SECURITY."

THE BAG CONTAINS ONE COMPUTER..."PENTIUM" PROCESSOR... ONE GIG HARD DRIVE... HIGHLY FRAGMENTED...

PLEASE WAIT WHILE I OPTIMIZE YOUR HARD DISK...

THIS IS VAGUELY UNSETTLING.

DO YOU SEE "TIME" AS A SEQUENCE OF DISCRETE EVENTS OR SIMPLY A LINE OF PERCEPTION THROUGH INFINITE POSSIBILITIES?

TECH EE

I SEE "TIME" AS MORE OF A MAGAZINE.

TECH EE

YOU KNOW THESE MOMENTS WE HAVE TOGETHER—WE REALLY MUST HAVE THEM LESS OFTEN.

ASK ME ABOUT "LIFE."

ALTHOUGH WE ARE NOTHING BUT POND SCUM IN THIS COMPANY...

IT'S NICE TO KNOW WE CAN STILL FIND SOMEONE OF LOWER STATUS TO TORMENT.

YOU CALL THESE BROCHURES? HOW CAN I EVEN CONSIDER BUYING PRODUCTS FROM A "VEN-DUH" SUCH AS YOU?

TELL ME IF THIS HURTS.

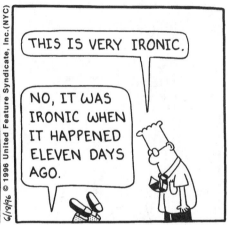

99

ALICE, I NEED TO GATHER SOME REQUIREMENTS BEFORE DESIGNING THE COMPANY CHILD CARE FACILITY.

DO YOU MIND IF YOUR CHILDREN SPEND THE DAY SEWING GARMENTS IN A WINDOWLESS ROOM FULL OF ILLEGAL ALIENS?

I MIND.

I'LL PUT YOU DOWN AS A MAYBE.

WOULD I GET DISCOUNTS ON THOSE GARMENTS?

HERE'S MY FINAL PLAN FOR THE COMPANY'S DAY CARE FACILITY.

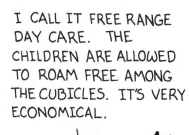

I CALL IT FREE RANGE DAY CARE. THE CHILDREN ARE ALLOWED TO ROAM FREE AMONG THE CUBICLES. IT'S VERY ECONOMICAL.

I DON'T BELIEVE HE'S REALLY AN EVIL TROLL.

LOOK AT THE "POWERPOINT" SLIDES HE'S MAKING. IT'S NOT HUMAN.

THE RESULTS OF THE EMPLOYEE SATISFACTION SURVEY ARE IN. SCORES FOR MY DEPARTMENT ARE DISMAL.

I'M ASSIGNING YOU TO THE SATISFACTION TASK FORCE UNTIL THE PROBLEM IS SOLVED.

PLEASE... ANYTHING BUT THAT...

HOW SATISFIED ARE YOU NOW?

102

RATBERT, MY COMPANY IS HIRING FOR OUR QUALITY ASSURANCE GROUP. YOU'D BE PERFECT.

WHAT WOULD I HAVE TO DO?

YOU WOULD FIND FLAWS IN OUR NEW PRODUCT, THUS MAKING YOURSELF AN OBJECT OF INTENSE HATRED AND RIDICULE.

BUT THEN YOU'D FIX THOSE FLAWS... AND YOUR RESPECT FOR ME WOULD GROW INTO A SPECIAL BOND OF FRIENDSHIP, RIGHT?!

NO, THEN WE SHIP.

I'D BE PERFECT FOR THE JOB IN QUALITY ASSURANCE. HERE'S MY RESUME.

ARE YOU BOTHERED BY THE FACT THAT HALF OF YOUR WORDS ARE SPELLED WRONG?

NOPE! I'M NOT EVEN BOTHERED BY YOUR ANAL-RETENTIVE BEHAVIOR.

YOU'RE HIRED. YOUR BONUS WILL EQUAL NEGATIVE 100% OF YOUR BASE SALARY. OKAY?

I DON'T SEE ANY PROBLEM WITH THAT.

MY QUALITY ASSURANCE REVIEW OF YOUR BETA PRODUCT TURNED UP A FEW BUGS, WALLY.

I'VE CLASSIFIED THE BUGS BY SEVERITY: 1) LETHAL, 2) BONEHEADED, 3) VEXING.

ALL I SEE ARE LETHAL AND VEXING. WHERE'S BONEHEADED?

I'M TRYING TO RENT A STADIUM TO HOLD THE PRINTOUT.

IN THE SHORT TIME YOU'VE WORKED IN QUALITY ASSURANCE, YOU'VE FOUND A HUGE NUMBER OF FLAWS IN OUR PROTOTYPE.

THAT'S MY JOB!

YOU'RE JEOPARDIZING OUR SCHEDULE. THE ENTIRE PROJECT WILL FAIL AND IT'S ALL YOUR FAULT.

WHY IS IT MY FAULT?

IF A TREE FALLS IN THE FOREST... AND WE'VE ALREADY SOLD THE TREE... DOES IT HAVE QUALITY?

HOW MANY ANGELS CAN DANCE ON YOUR HEAD?

LET'S HAVE A LITTLE PREMEETING TO PREPARE FOR THE MEETING TOMORROW.

WHOA! DO YOU THINK IT'S SAFE TO JUMP RIGHT INTO THE PREMEETING WITHOUT PLANNING IT?

OKAY, LET'S GET THIS PRELIMINARY PREMEETING MEETING GOING.

YOU THINK YOU'RE FUNNY, BUT YOU'RE NOT.

I COULDN'T HELP NOTICING THE BUGS IN THE PROGRAM ON THIS OLD DISKETTE YOU THREW AWAY.

I FIXED THE BUGS AND TIGHTENED THE CODE FROM TWELVE THOUSAND LINES TO SIXTEEN.

IT TOOK ME THREE MONTHS TO WRITE THAT PROGRAM.

I TOOK THE LIBERTY OF UPDATING YOUR RESUME. I'M GUESSING YOU'LL NEED IT SOON.

SOMEDAY WHEN I BECOME THE SUPREME RULER OF EARTH...

I'LL ORDER EVERYBODY TO GO OUTSIDE ONCE A DAY AND RUN AROUND WITH THEIR MOUTHS OPEN.

BECAUSE YOU SUPPORT FRESH AIR AND EXERCISE?

BECAUSE I HATE FLIES.

THANKS FOR MAKING THAT PRODUCT MOCK-UP LAST WEEK. THE CUSTOMER LIKED IT SO MUCH THAT HE ORDERED A THOUSAND!

THAT WAS A **MOCK-UP**! WE DON'T MAKE THAT PRODUCT YET. IT WOULD TAKE THREE YEARS TO MAKE ONE.

JUST GIVE ME A THOUSAND MOCK-UPS. THE FIRST ONE WAS TERRIFIC!

THE MOCK-UP WAS OUR COMPETITOR'S PRODUCT WITH DUCT TAPE OVER THE LOGO.

I'LL NEED YOUR FULL MANAGEMENT SUPPORT IN THIS MEETING WITH SALES.

JUST WATCH THE MASTER AT WORK.

I PROMISED A CUSTOMER A PRODUCT THAT WE DON'T MAKE. YOU NEED TO ENGINEER-UP A THOUSAND UNITS BY EARLY NEXT WEEK.

IS THURSDAY OKAY?

WAIT UNTIL HE FINDS OUT THAT THURSDAY ISN'T "EARLY NEXT WEEK." HEE HEE!

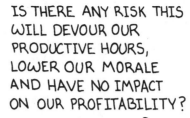

CATBERT, THE EVIL DIRECTOR OF HUMAN RESOURCES

ACCORDING TO MY SOURCES, YOU'VE BEEN ENJOYING YOUR JOB, WALLY.

IT WAS TEMPORARY. I DON'T KNOW WHAT GOT INTO ME...

PLEASE REFER TO PAGE ONE OF THE EMPLOYEE MANUAL.

"JOB SATISFACTION IS THE SAME AS STEALING FROM THE COMPANY." I'LL HAVE TO CHARGE YOU FOR ADMISSION UNLESS I START HEARING SOME SHRIEKS OF PAIN.

IN THE YEAR THAT WE'VE DATED, LIZ, YOU'VE OFTEN MENTIONED VARIOUS PROBLEMS IN YOUR LIFE.

I HAVE COMPILED THOSE PROBLEMS INTO A LIST OF REQUIREMENTS AND DEVELOPED A COMPREHENSIVE SET OF SOLUTIONS.

HOW THOUGHTFUL. I DIDN'T EVEN KNOW I WAS BROKEN.

NO, NO, NOT BROKEN... JUST A BIT BUGGY.

UM... WHEN I'VE SHARED MY FEELINGS WITH YOU, I WASN'T HOPING YOU'D DESIGN AN ACTION PLAN TO SOLVE ALL OF MY PROBLEMS.

WHY ELSE WOULD YOU TELL ME ALL OF YOUR PROBLEMS... UNLESS IT'S SOME DEMENTED PLOT TO MAKE YOURSELF FEEL BETTER AT MY EXPENSE?

YOU WERE RIGHT. IT WAS ALL A DEMENTED PLOT.

I'M TRYING TO GRADUALLY LIFT YOUR VEIL OF IGNORANCE.

OUR NEW "RECOGNITION PROGRAM" ASSIGNS THE NAMES OF PRECIOUS GEMS TO YOUR LEVELS OF PERFORMANCE.

THE HIGHEST LEVEL IS DIAMOND. YOU GET A NEW RING AT EACH LEVEL.

ARE YOU SURE TALC IS A PRECIOUS GEM?

I THINK I SAW IT SPARKLE.

AS YOU CAN SEE FROM MY RING, I'M A MEMBER OF THE "TALC CLUB" AT WORK.

WITH HARD WORK AND A BIT OF LUCK I WILL RISE TO THE NEXT LEVEL: SHALE.

I CAN HONESTLY SAY MY RESPECT FOR YOU HAS NEVER BEEN HIGHER.

SOMEDAY, GOD WILLING, I'LL MAKE IT TO ALUMINUM.

IT'S TIME FOR ME TO UPDATE YOUR OBJECTIVES, ALICE.

WE NEED TARGETS THAT CAN ONLY BE ACHIEVED BY AMAZINGLY HARD WORK PLUS THE CONSTANT SUPPORT OF MANAGEMENT.

I'M BUSY, SO YOU'LL HAVE TO WRITE THEM YOURSELF.

WHAT'S WRONG WITH THIS PICTURE?

IT LOOKS LIKE WE'LL RELEASE OUR NEW PRODUCT ON TIME, DESPITE ITS MANY DEFECTS.

WE'VE MINIMIZED THE ECONOMIC IMPACT OF THE DEFECTS VIA AN ADVANCED BUSINESS PROCESS CALLED "HOPING NOBODY NOTICES."

AND WE'VE DOUBLED OUR PROJECTED INCOME BY MODIFYING OUR ASSUMPTIONS!

A LOT OF THIS JOB IS MENTAL.

HERE IN THE "DOGBERT INSTITUTE FOR ADVANCED THINKING," I HAVE DEVISED A PLAN FOR ENDING POVERTY.

MY PLAN IS TO WAIT UNTIL THERE ARE SO MANY TALK SHOWS ON TELEVISION THAT ALL THE PEOPLE WITH WRETCHED LIVES CAN BE PAID GUESTS.

WHAT ABOUT THE POOR PEOPLE WHO DON'T WANT TO BE ON TALK SHOWS?

WE'LL GET THE STRAGGLERS ON "COPS."

FROM NOW ON, I WILL NOT TRY TO REASON WITH THE IDIOTS I ENCOUNTER. I WILL DISMISS THEM BY WAVING MY PAW AND SAYING "BAH."

JUST BECAUSE SOMEONE THINKS DIFFERENTLY FROM YOU DOESN'T MEAN HE'S AN IDIOT, DOGBERT.

BAH.

THE VOTES ARE IN. I'VE BEEN ELECTED TO THE POSITION OF SUPREME RULER OF EARTH.

I WON IN A LANDSLIDE, THANKS TO LOW VOTER TURNOUT AND THE FACT THAT I VOTED FOR MYSELF MANY TIMES.

I HOPE YOU'LL BE A BENEVOLENT RULER.

I THINK I'LL MAKE CANING AN OLYMPIC EVENT.

MY DOMINION OVER THE PLANET IS NOT WIDELY RECOGNIZED BY THE DOLTS WHO ARE BREATHING MY AIR.

SO I'VE DECLARED TOTAL SOVEREIGNTY OVER A SMALL, EVER-WIDENING ZONE SURROUNDING MY BODY.

HOW BIG IS THE ZONE?

YOU HAVE JUST ENTERED DOGBERT-LAND. PLEASE SHOW YOUR PASSPORT AND LEAVE THE OXYGEN ALONE!

IF WE ARE TO SUCCEED, YOU MUST BECOME CHANGE MASTERS IN AN EVER-CHANGING, CHANGE-ADAPTIVE ENVIRONMENT.

LET ME GET THIS STRAIGHT... EVERY CHANGE SEEMS TO INCREASE OUR WORKLOAD WHILE DECREASING OUR JOB SECURITY AND REAL EARNINGS AFTER INFLATION...

AND THE PROBLEM IS OUR LACK OF FLEXIBILITY?

NOT ENTIRELY. THERE'S ALSO YOUR BAD MORALE.

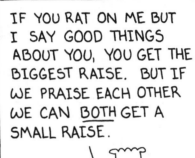

120

DOGBERT: CAREER COUNSELOR

I WAS FIRED ONCE, BUT I CAME BACK AS A CONTRACT EMPLOYEE. LATER I WAS REHIRED AT A HIGHER SALARY.

NOW I'M BEING DOWN-SIZED AGAIN. DO YOU THINK THEY'LL BE DUMB ENOUGH TO HIRE ME A THIRD TIME?

YOUR STORY REMINDS ME OF THE PARABLE OF THE ANT AND THE SPIDER.

REALLY? HOW?

THEY'RE BOTH BORING.

DOGBERT: CAREER COUNSELOR

THE COMPANY WON'T LAY YOU OFF IF ENOUGH PEOPLE QUIT FIRST.

YOUR BEST STRATEGY IS TO CONVINCE YOUR CO-WORKERS THAT THEIR JOBS ARE INTOLERABLE.

WE DO THIS FOR ALL THE YOUNG EMPLOYEES, ASOK. I'LL CAPTURE ON VIDEO THE EXACT MOMENT THAT YOUR LIFE FORCE LEAVES YOUR BODY.

GOOD NEWS, WALLY. MOST OF OUR SMART EMPLOYEES QUIT TO GET MUCH BETTER JOBS ELSEWHERE. NOW WE DON'T HAVE TO DO ANY DOWNSIZING.

YOUR JOB IS SAFE. WE NEED YOU TO DO THE WORK OF ALL THE PEOPLE WHO LEFT.

IS IT JUST ME... OR IS THE QUALITY OF "GOOD NEWS" REALLY GOING DOWNHILL LATELY?

I'D HAVE TO SAY YOU'RE BOTH GOING DOWNHILL.

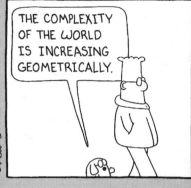

I AM ONLY A LOWLY INTERN, BUT I SEE AN OBVIOUS SOLUTION TO YOUR PROBLEM.

JUST CLICK HERE... CLEAR YOUR BUFFERS AND INITIALIZE THE LINK... NOW USE THIS CODE PATCH FOR THE MEMORY LEAK.

THIS IS FUNNY IF YOU CONSIDER THAT YOUR SALARY IS TWICE AS MUCH AS MINE.

I'M LAUGHING ON THE INSIDE.

ASOK THE INTERN

I CAME IN OVER THE WEEKEND AND LOOKED AT THE DESIGN YOU'VE BEEN WORKING WITH ALL YEAR.

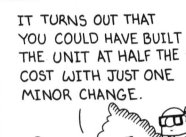

IT TURNS OUT THAT YOU COULD HAVE BUILT THE UNIT AT HALF THE COST WITH JUST ONE MINOR CHANGE.

IS IT TRUE I CAN WIN AWARDS FOR THIS SORT OF THING?

FETCH THE INTERNAPULT.

I'M GOING TO USE BAD GRAMMAR MORE OFTEN.

MY LEADERSHIP WILL CHANGE THE LANGUAGE THROUGH THE PRINCIPLE OF COMMON USAGE.

AND I WON'T STOP UNTIL THE ENTIRE LANGUAGE IS REDUCED TO GRUNTING AND POINTING! BUWAHA-HAHA!!

I REALLY GOT RIPPED OFF BY THAT DOG OBEDIENCE SCHOOL.

CATBERT THE HR DIRECTOR

MORALE IS LOW BECAUSE THE EMPLOYEES ARE UNDERPAID.

YOU CAN COMPENSATE BY HAVING MORE FREQUENT PERFORMANCE REVIEWS. THEY LOVE FEEDBACK.

THE HARDEST PART IS KEEPING A STRAIGHT FACE.

TELL ME AGAIN WHY I'D WANT MORALE TO BE HIGH?

GOOD NEWS, ALICE. I'M GOING TO HAVE QUARTERLY PERFORMANCE REVIEWS TO BOOST MORALE.

WOW! IN ADDITION TO WORKING SIXTEEN HOURS A DAY IN THIS BIG BOX, NOW I'LL GET 300% MORE CRITICISM!

I'LL HAVE A CHANCE TO HEAR EMPLOYEE CONCERNS FOUR TIMES A YEAR.

I ASSUME COMPREHENSION WILL REMAIN ON THE BICENTENNIAL PLAN.

AT FIRST I THOUGHT YOU COMMITTED ME TO AN IMPOSSIBLE DEADLINE. BUT I HAVE A THEORETICAL SOLUTION.

IT INVOLVES FLYING AROUND THE EARTH SO FAST THAT I TRAVEL BACK TO THE PAST.

AND THEN YOU'LL HAVE ENOUGH TIME?

NO, THEN I'LL GIVE YOUR PARENTS THIS PAMPHLET ON CONTRACEPTION.